# A PARTRIDGE IN

# A PARTRIDGE IN A PEAR TREE

*Poems For The Twelve Days Of Christmas*

by

# JOHN HEATH-STUBBS

*Illustrations by Emily Johns*

*Hearing Eye*

Winter 1988/1989

ISBN 1 870841 06 9 (hardback edition)
ISBN 1 870841 07 7 (paperback edition)

Published by Hearing Eye,
Box No. 1, 99 Torriano Avenue,
London NW5.
Printed by Aldgate Press, E1

Printed in London in an edition of 1,000 copies of which 1-50 will be signed by the author.

*On the first day of Christmas my true love sent to me...*

## A PARTRIDGE IN A PEAR TREE

A partridge perched on a pear-tree bough

On Christmas day – *une jolie perdriz*:

She had grown plump on stubble-gleaning

In September, and had dodged the guns.


Bare the branches now, but when spring comes

Leaves shall deck them and at summer's close

Depending pears, great tears of musky sweetness.

*On the second day of Christmas my true love sent to me...*

## TWO TURTLE DOVES

I send the image of two turtle-doves,

A token of fidelity. They do not flutter here

In cold December, under English skies.

In due time they'll be back with other migrants

From climes more southerly. First will come the chiffchaff;

Then in May

The laggard fern-owl and the tardy turtle:

*Tur-tur, tur-tur, tur-tur*, be heard

About the land, a soft murmuring,

Amid profusion of the spring-time flowers.

*On the third day of Christmas my true love sent to me…*

## THREE FRENCH HENS

Honorine, Alphonsine, and Pertelot –

Three French hens, scrabble and scrape

For groundsel and ground-ivy in the gravel.

They cluck and chuckle disapprovingly

About *ce méchant Monsieur Chanticler*

And all his goings-on; the *affreuse* malice

Of that hunchbacked guinea-fowl,

Her widow's black sewn with pearls for tears;

And that canard canaille,

The waddling and mud-dabbling ducks and ducklings.

*On the fourth day of Christmas my true love sent to me…*

## FOUR CALLING BIRDS

Four birds calling and crying

In December twilight –

Four colly birds, four coal-black blackbirds –

*'Tack, tack, tack, tack, tack!'*

Through the leafless wood, till roosting time.

*On the fifth day of Christmas my true love sent to me...*

FIVE GOLD RINGS

Five golden circles wed

Your senses to the outer world. One is for sight –

Sun-rays, marigold, fields of oil-seed rape,

The yellowhammer's feathers, eyes

Of lace-wing and of gadfly. One is for sound –

Gold blare of the trumpet, harp strings,

Gold-billed blackbird's song, and voices

Of those you loved, in dreams. And one for scent –

Perfume of mignonette,

And of the gorse that blooms on the summer heath,

And brandy-bottle yellow water-lily.

One for all rich and exquisite flavours –

Buttered haddock, Gloucester cheese, omelettes,

Pamplemousse, honey, saffron cake. And one

For the cold hard feel you get from gold itself.

*On the sixth day of Christmas my true love sent to me...*

## SIX GEESE A-LAYING

Six geese stepping upon the green,

Honking and hissing – they will scare away

All the tedious and quotidian devils

That fret at your life, or cling to it like goose-grass

(Juno's geese it was that saved the Capitol)

And, if you're very lucky,

Before the year is over,

There's one that's going to lay the alchemical egg.

*On the seventh day of Christmas my true love sent to me...*

## SEVEN SWANS A-SWIMMING

Seven wild swans are floating

Under a bleak sky, over a waste sea.

Another year comes round, and still

No end to their continual exile here.


These are Lir's children, changed

To wild whooping swans, that whistling call

Their desolate lament. Only a Christian bell, a hermit's bell

Chiming for matins or for evensong

Over the noisy waves, shall break

That black enchantment and restore them

To human form, human companionship.

*On the eighth day of Christmas my true love sent to me...*

## EIGHT MAIDS A-MILKING

"Where are you going, this frosty morning,

My eight mawthers?"   "To the cattle-byre.

Our cows need milking – Dapple and Whitesocks,

Buttercup, Moondaisy, Tulip and Sorrel,

Periwinkle and Crumplehorn. The milk and the cream

Are wanted for junkets and syllabubs,

Cheesecakes and flummery, for the Twelfth Night feast –

It's not far off now."

*On the ninth day of Christmas my true love sent to me...*

## NINE LADIES DANCING

They dance by the frozen lake, a silver mirror

For the great winter moon and for the stars.

Their dance is light and darkness, day and night-time,

Winter and spring, the summer and the autumn,

Man's birth, man's life, man's death – they are nine witches,

Nine white witches in a shining midnight.

*On the tenth day of Christmas my true love sent to me…*

## TEN LORDS A-LEAPING

Ten lords come rushing in, tripping and skipping;

Kicking up their heels they whoop and halloo.

Each takes a lady by the hand – there are nine ladies:

Lord Prance, Lord Hopfrog, and Lord Salar Salmon,

Lord Jiminy Cricket, and Lord Merryrig,

All choose their partners – so do brisk Lord Wallaby,

Lord Capriole, Lord Pulex, and Lord Highjump.

One, two, three, hop! – see them dance the polka,

Lavolta, piedz-en-l'air and saltarello,

Trepaks and gopaks – all the jumping dances!

There's only one lord cannot find a lady –

Lord Oddmanout – and he must leap alone.

*On the eleventh day of Christmas my true love sent to me…*

## ELEVEN PIPERS PIPING

Eleven shepherds piped around a manger.

Eleven days have passed, and they must take their leave.

Their bagpipe tunes are fading, as they go

Back to the high hills, where linger still

Reverberations of the angels' song.

*On the twelfth day of Christmas my true love sent to me...*

## TWELVE DRUMMERS DRUMMING

Twelve drummers, twelve African drummers:
Ostrich plumes nod over their locks;
Lion skins and monkey tails drape
Their naked shoulders; barbaric blazing rubies
Gleam on the shining blackness of their chests.

Three kings march towards Bethlehem,
With gifts of gold and spices, and the third
Is Balthasar of Ethiopia
With his medicine-herb. These are his entourage;
Their talking rhythms make articulate
Surge of the blood, the rising of the sap,
A sacrificial dance of death in spring,
Thunder of resurrection, and beyond it
The rushing of a pentecostal wind.

Also published by Hearing Eye:

John Heath-Stubbs:
Cats' Parnassus (1987)
Time Pieces (1988)
Both with illustrations by Emily Johns.